Hamlet

Classroom Questions

A SCENE BY SCENE TEACHING GUIDE

Amy Farrell

SCENE BY SCENE

ENNISKERRY, IRELAND

Scene by Scene
11 Millfield, Enniskerry
Wicklow, Ireland.
www.scenebysceneguides.com

Hamlet Scene by Scene Classroom Questions/Amy Farrell. —1st ed.
ISBN 978-1-910949-23-8

Contents

Contents

Act One, Scene One

Points to Consider

• Students will understand and follow this scene best if you prepare them by explaining what is about to happen. This lets them follow the storyline more easily and prepares them for the apparition of the Ghost of Old Hamlet.

• This scene introduces Horatio as a learned and respected character.

• We are given the background to the political situation in Denmark and the threat of Norway.

Questions

1. What is going on as the play begins?

2. Why has Horatio been asked to attend the watch?

3. What unusual sight do the men see?

4. What reason does Horatio give for this "strict and most observant watch"? (line 71)

5. What do the men decide to do as the scene ends?

Act One, Scene Two

Points to Consider

● Students tend to find the marriage of Gertrude and Claudius to be quite sensational and scandalous, particularly considering how recently King Hamlet has died.

● Claudius appears as a competent monarch in this scene, handling matters of state with confidence. He is particularly gracious to Laertes, Polonius' son, something worth pointing out to students, so they are aware of the relationship between the new King and Polonius.

● Students tend to respond positively to Hamlet in this scene; they like his wit and understand why he feels so affronted by his mother's behaviour. Although he is in a dark, depressed mood, most students recognise why he is feeling this way, and don't judge him negatively for it. His willingness to attend the watch in search of his father's ghost also tends to win him admiration from students.

● This scene interests students both from the supernatural point of view, and also from the perspective of Gertrude's marriage to Claudius.

Questions

1. What information does Claudius reveal in his opening speech?

2. What does Laertes want from Claudius?

3. What kind of mood is Hamlet in when we first meet him?

4. How well do Claudius and Hamlet get on?

5. What do the King and Queen want Hamlet to do in this scene?

6. How does Hamlet feel about his mother's marriage to Claudius?

7. What news does Horatio bring Hamlet?

8. What does Hamlet plan to do and why does he do this?

Act One, Scene Three

Points to Consider

• This scene introduces the romantic plotline to the drama, that of the relationship between Ophelia and Hamlet. Ophelia's brother and father both warn her to stay clear of Hamlet, and she consents to do so. Students may question her willingness to forsake the prince, suggesting that she may not truly love him. This in turn, may lead to a discussion of family loyalty and obedience.

Questions

1.   What advice does Laertes give his sister, Ophelia, about Hamlet?

2.   What advice does Polonius give his son?

3.   What does Ophelia reveal to her father about her relationship with Hamlet?

4.   How does Polonius treat his daughter?

5.   What are your first impressions of Ophelia?

6.   What does Polonius think of Hamlet?

Act One, Scene Four

Points to Consider

●   Hamlet's poor view of his uncle is further developed in this scene, as he disapproves of his drunkenness.

●   Hamlet shows himself to be a thoughtful, deep thinking young man. He appears to be depressed, placing little value on his life, and fearlessly follows his father's ghost, despite the warnings of the other men. It can be interesting to discuss what students would do in his position, and whether they would follow the ghostly apparition.

Questions

1.   Describe the atmosphere as this scene begins.

2.   Does Hamlet approve of his uncle's drunken revelry?

3.   What makes Hamlet speak to the Ghost?

4.   Why do the other men try to prevent Hamlet from speaking with the Ghost?

5.   Describe Hamlet's character, based on what you have seen of him so far.

Act One, Scene Five

Points to Consider

●   This is a very exciting scene in the play, as students learn of the murder of Old Hamlet at his brother's hands, and the quest for vengeance that falls to Hamlet. The knowledge that is revealed to Hamlet by the Ghost will be the basis for most of the action that is to follow.

●   Hamlet claims that he will use the appearance of madness to his advantage towards the end of this scene. This is worth noting, as it will aid future discussions of Hamlet's mental state.

Questions

1. What does the Ghost reveal to Hamlet and what does he want Hamlet to do?

2. How did Claudius kill the King?

3. What does the Ghost say about Hamlet's mother, Gertrude?

4. How does Hamlet react to what the Ghost tells him?

5. What does Hamlet get his friends to agree to as the scene closes?

Act Two, Scene One

Points to Consider

●   Polonius is revealed as a devious, cunning character, when he explains to Reynaldo the methods he wants him to use to spy on his son, Laertes. This tends to shock and even outrage some students, who are taken aback at this treatment.

●   Students may find it frustrating that Ophelia went straight to her father after Hamlet sought her out in such a distressed state. They may feel that her loyalty and obedience to her father has cost Hamlet the only comfort and understanding he may have had. Again, the question of whether she truly loves him may arise in discussion.

Questions

1. What does Polonius want Reynaldo to do?

2. Why does he want him to do this?

3. Do you think it is right that Polonius should treat his son in this way?

4. What has "affrighted" Ophelia?

5. What reason does Polonius offer for Hamlet's behaviour?

6. Why do you think Hamlet visited Ophelia at this point?

7. What are your views on Ophelia at this stage?

Act Two, Scene Two

Points to Consider

• Claudius is aware of Hamlet's strange behaviour and intends to use his friends, Rosencrantz and Guildenstern, to find out what is up with him. Students tend to view this as a sneaky, conniving betrayal on Claudius' part, and are often disappointed when the prince's friends readily acquiesce. It may be necessary to stress Claudius' powerful position at court to help students fully understand the predicament that Hamlet's friends find themselves in, although they are by no means blameless themselves.

• Gertrude, unlike Claudius and Polonius, realises the true cause of her son's low mood, "His father's death and our o'erhasty marriage". This suggests a closeness and true understanding of her son.

• Polonius' plan to spy on Hamlet further establishes him as a deceitful character.

• Hamlet's wit in speaking with Polonius shows he is a clever, sharp character. Students tend to like him for this, and feel sorry for him in his troubled, depressed state. Polonius' slow-wittedness and inability to understand Hamlet's remarks will further diminish him in their eyes.

●   Hamlet's response to the news of the Players shows a different side to his character. He appears enthusiastic and sociable. On a serious note, the play will give Hamlet the opportunity to gather the proof he needs against Claudius.

Questions

1. What does Claudius want Rosencrantz and Guildenstern to do for him?

2. What does Gertrude consider the cause of Hamlet's upset to be?

3. What news does Voltemand bring the King?

4. What does Polonius tell the King and Queen about Hamlet?

5. What plan has Polonius devised to find out whether Hamlet's madness is to do with Ophelia?

6. How does Hamlet's mood change when he first meets his friends, Rosencrantz and Guildenstern?

7. What reason do his friends find for Hamlet thinking, "Denmark's a prison"?

8. What does Hamlet reveal to Rosencrantz and Guildenstern about his state of mind?

9. How does Hamlet react to news of the Players arriving at the court?

10. What view of old age is given in this scene and what is the effect of this?

11. How does Hamlet treat Polonius?

12. What is Hamlet's attitude to drama?

13. What is significant about the First Player's speech?

14. Why is Hamlet annoyed with himself as this scene ends?

15. What are Hamlet's concerns about the Ghost?

16. What does Hamlet hope to achieve by staging this play?

Act Three, Scene One

Points to Consider

● Polonius and Claudius now try to discover the cause of Hamlet's strange behaviour, by setting him up and spying on how he reacts to Ophelia, something that generally angers students as they view it as unfair and deceitful.

● Hamlet is in a troubled, philosophical mood as he enters this scene. It can be worth discussing why he is feeling this way and how well he is perceived to be coping.

● Hamlet treats Ophelia with scorn and cruelty in this scene, perhaps misdirecting anger intended for his mother towards her (his comments are quite damning of women). However, her compliance in Polonius' set-up here means that some students will have little sympathy for her, claiming that she is part of the reason that Hamlet feels as he does. Often, she is judged negatively for being too obedient and willing to help her devious father.

● As the scene ends, Claudius and Polonius scheme how best to get Hamlet out of the way. This increases the tension, and student support for the young prince.

Questions

1. As this scene opens, how does Claudius speak of Hamlet's state of mind?

2. What are Polonius and Claudius planning to do?

3. What is the Queen's attitude to Ophelia?

4. What is Hamlet thinking about as he enters this scene and what does it tell us about him?

5. Why does Hamlet tell Ophelia to "Get thee to a nunnery"?

6. What does Hamlet think of Polonius?

7. Describe Hamlet's views on love and marriage and explain why he feels this way.

8. In your opinion, why does Hamlet treat Ophelia so cruelly in this scene?

9. What different plans do Claudius and Polonius come up with for dealing with Hamlet?

Act Three, Scene Two

Points to Consider

• Hamlet confides in Horatio in this scene and asks him to observe Claudius for signs of guilt.

• Hamlet feels his suspicions are justified when he sees Claudius' guilty reaction to the murder on-stage. He is now convinced that the Ghost has told him the truth.

• Hamlet speaks sharply to Ophelia, and some students may feel sorry for her when they see this, feeling that she had to obey Polonius and act as she did.

• Hamlet reacts angrily when he realises his friends, Rosencrantz and Guildenstern, have been relaying information back to the King. He is becoming increasingly isolated as the play progresses.

Questions

1.   What is Hamlet's opinion of Horatio?

2.   What does Hamlet ask Horatio to do for him during the insert-play?

3.   What happens in the dumb-show?

4.   How does Hamlet treat Ophelia as they prepare to watch the players?

5.   What views on re-marrying does the Player Queen reveal as the play begins? Whose views are these really?

6.   Is the Player King convinced by his wife?

7.   From Hamlet's viewpoint, is the play a success?

8.   What do you think of Claudius' reaction to the play?

9.   Why does Hamlet treat Rosencrantz coolly in this scene?

10. What is Hamlet's problem with Guildenstern?

11. Describe Hamlet's mood as the scene ends.

Act Three, Scene Three

Points to Consider

• King Claudius feels threatened by Hamlet and intends to ship him off to England, accompanied by Rosencrantz and Guildenstern. This increases the tension, as it is an obvious move against the Prince.

• In this scene, Claudius reveals his guilt in soliloquy. He is suffering because of his wrongdoing, and is incapable of prayer, but cannot seek forgiveness, as he is unwilling to give up his ill-gotten crown or his wife.

• Hamlet enters the King's chamber, intent on killing him, but thinks the King is praying because he is on his knees. Unwilling to send him to the next world with a clear conscience, he postpones killing him until a later date. This is something students will want to discuss, with many feeling that this failed opportunity indicates weakness in Hamlet.

Questions

1. What does the King intend to do about Hamlet?

2. How are Rosencrantz and Guildenstern reacting to the King's fear?

3. What do you think of Polonius' offer to spy on Hamlet and Gertrude?

4. How does Claudius feel about the crime he has committed?

5. What does Hamlet intend to do when he finds Claudius alone?

6. Why doesn't Hamlet kill Claudius on this occasion?

7. Do you believe his reasons for sparing the King are genuine?

Act Three, Scene Four

Points to Consider

• Hamlet kills Polonius in this scene, mistakenly thinking that it was the King who hid and spied on him. This act will have significant consequences for Hamlet (Laertes' quest for vengeance, Ophelia's drowning), while also adding excitement to the scene itself.

• Hamlet speaks viciously and openly to his mother in this scene, something that provokes strong reactions in students. Some will feel that Gertrude deserves this harsh treatment, while others will feel that she is not afforded the respect due to her from her son.

Questions

1. What does Polonius do as the scene begins?

2. How does Hamlet speak to his mother as she begins to chastise him for his behaviour?

3. Why does Hamlet kill Polonius?

4. Do you think Hamlet is too cold and harsh in this scene?

5. Why doesn't Hamlet believe that his mother loves Claudius?

6. Describe Hamlet's treatment of his mother in this scene.

7. Based on this scene, do you think Gertrude committed adultery and was an accomplice in Old Hamlet's murder?

8. How does Hamlet describe his mother's relationship with Claudius?

9. What impact does Hamlet's speech have on Gertrude?

10. Do you think Hamlet regrets killing Polonius? Explain.

Act Four, Scene One

Points to Consider

• Students often react negatively towards Gertrude because she wastes no time in telling Claudius about Hamlet's rash slaying of Polonius. Therefore, it is important to point out that she prefaces her statement by stressing Hamlet's madness, perhaps in an attempt to protect her son. She doesn't pretend that he is feigning madness and even claims that he is feeling remorseful, which he has shown no sign of.

• Claudius immediately thinks of his own safety when he hears what Hamlet has done, and intends to ship him off to England without delay.

Questions

1.   Does Gertrude protect her son in this scene?

2.   What are Claudius' concerns when he learns of Polonius' death?

Act Four, Scene Two

Points to Consider

●   In this scene Hamlet acts the part of a lunatic, leading his pursuers to chase him around the castle. It may be viewed as black humour, considering he has just killed Polonius.

Questions

1.   How does Hamlet treat Rosencrantz?

2.   Hamlet behaves like a man who has lost his reason.
       Do you think he has? Explain.

3.   What will people think of Hamlet?

4.   How does this scene end?

Act Four, Scene Three

Points to Consider

• Hamlet's hiding of Polonius' corpse and the black humour he engages in is quite dark, something that students tend to react to.

• While few will be surprised by Claudius' murder plans for his nephew, most will be outraged that this is what he plans to do.

Questions

1.   How does Claudius view his nephew?

2.   What has Hamlet done with Polonius' corpse?
      What is your reponse to this?

3.   What is Claudius planning for Hamlet in England?
      Why doesn't this take place in Denmark?
      What does this tell you about Claudius' character?

Act Four, Scene Four

Points to Consider

●   Hamlet responds to the news of Fortinbras' military campaign by pledging to become a man of action, rather than a man of thoughts and words. This reminds us that he still intends to seek revenge, as instructed by his father's Ghost.

Questions

1. Why has Fortinbras gone to war?

2. What reason does Hamlet give for this conflict?

3. How does Hamlet react to Fortinbras' military campaign?

4. Does Hamlet see this war as something worthwhile and honourable?

5. What does Hamlet reveal to us in soliloquy as this scene ends?

Act Four, Scene Five

Points to Consider

•   Ophelia is a pathetic character in this scene, driven to madness by her father's death and the unhappy end to her relationship with Hamlet. There may be a mixed response in students' views on Ophelia at this stage; some will sympathise, while others may feel she brought some of her misfortune on herself.

•   Claudius manipulates and uses Laertes in this scene. He cunningly wields the young man's grief as a way to control him.

•   Students should notice both the parallels and differences between Laertes and Hamlet in how they are dealing with their fathers' murders and how they seek retribution.

Questions

1.   How is Ophelia behaving, according to the gentleman?

2.   Describe Gertrude's mood as the scene begins.

3.   What is the significance of the songs Ophelia sings?

4.   Why is Ophelia so upset, in your opinion?

5.   What is the cause of Laertes' anger?

6.   What differences do you notice between Hamlet and
       Laertes in their attitudes to revenge?

7.   Do you think Claudius does a good job of handling Laertes?

8.   How does Laertes react when he sees his sister?

9.   Comment on the gifts of flowers Ophelia makes to
       Laertes, Gertrude and Claudius.

Act Four, Scene Six

Points to Consider

•   Some students will feel that Hamlet's rescue by pirates and secret return to Denmark is something of a cheat, particularly as it all occurs so quickly and neatly offstage. It may be necessary to stress that his speedy return, unknownst to his uncle, aids the dramatic tempo and development of the play.

Questions

1.   What does Hamlet's letter reveal?

2.   Hamlet doesn't mention where he's staying to Horatio.
        Why is this the case?

Act Four, Scene Seven

Points to Consider

●   Claudius showcases his cunning in this scene, as he expertly motivates and manipulates Laertes.

●   The news of Ophelia's death is another blow to Laertes, but it leaves Claudius unmoved.

Questions

1.   What excuses does Claudius give Laertes for not acting against Hamlet after Polonius' murder?

2.   Do you believe Claudius really loves Gertrude as he says he does? Explain your answer.

3.   How does Claudius react to Hamlet's letter?

4.   How does Laertes react to the news of Hamlet's arrival?

5.   How does Claudius use Laertes in this scene?

6.   What does Claudius say to make Laertes want to fence with Hamlet?

7.   What plan does Claudius put forward for killing Hamlet?

8.   Describe Laertes' character, as you see him.

9.   What has happened Ophelia?

10.   Do you think Claudius' moral decline worsens in this scene? Explain.

Act Five, Scene One

Points to Consider

• Many students will recognise aspects of this scene and will have seen re-workings of it. Therefore it may be worthwhile to discuss what they recognise.

• It can be worthwhile to discuss the setting and how it contributes to the atmosphere and mood in this scene.

• The theme of death features heavily in this scene, which is worth discussing.

• Hamlet appears to have changed since we last saw him; he appears calmer and more self-assured.

• Students tend to respond positively to Hamlet's declaration of love for Ophelia, while most will judge Laertes' show of grief to be over the top.

Questions

1.   What is happening as this scene begins?

2.   Briefly describe the conversation between the two gravediggers.

3.   What does the sight of the skull make Hamlet think of?

4.   Why is it significant that the gravedigger took up his trade on the day that Hamlet was born?

5.   What is significant about Hamlet finding the skull of Yorick in the graveyard?

6.   What reason does the priest give for Ophelia's incomplete funeral rites?

7.   What do you think of the fact that Laertes leaps into Ophelia's grave and asks to be buried with her?

8.   Comment on the line, "This is I, Hamlet the Dane".

9.   Hamlet claims, "I loved Ophelia". Is this true, in your opinion?

10. "O he is mad Laertes". Why does Claudius want Laertes to think Hamlet is mad?

11. The scene as a whole provides us with much to consider about Death. Discuss the main issues it raises.

Act Five, Scene Two

Points to Consider

●   Hamlet appears more accepting of Fate than in the earlier portions of the play.

●   The duel is a highpoint of the play. While they enjoy the excitement of it, some students will lament the fact that so many characters die in this final scene. It may be necessary to stress the theme of Death and the tragic nature of the play.

●   Students tend to react strongly to Claudius' half-hearted attempts to prevent Gertrude's poisoning.

●   It can be interesting to discuss and assess Hamlet's character, and his treatment of Laertes in particular, in this scene.

●   It is important to note that with the arrival of Fortinbras, a form of order is restored to the royal court.

Questions

1. What information does Hamlet give Horatio about his adventures at sea?

2. As the scene begins, do you notice any changes in Hamlet's character from earlier in the play?

3. How did Hamlet escape the death his uncle intended for him in England?

4. Do you think Hamlet has treated Rosencrantz and Guildenstern too harshly?

5. How does Hamlet treat Osric?

6. What wager has Claudius made?

7. How does Hamlet speak to Laertes before the duel? What does it show of his character?

8. "Gertrude, do not drink". Why does Claudius make such a half-hearted effort to prevent Gertrude from drinking from the poisoned cup?

9. "And yet it is almost against my conscience". What does Laertes' delay in striking Hamlet tell us?

10. Do you think this is a fitting end for Claudius?

11. As Hamlet dies, Horatio says, "Now cracks a noble heart". Is this an accurate comment, in your opinion?

12. Is there a major difference between Laertes and Claudius? Explain.

13. Do you feel sorry for Gertrude in this scene? Explain.

14. How has Hamlet developed throughout the play?

15. Comment on the state of Denmark as the play ends.

Visit www.scenebysceneguides.com to see our full catalogue of Classroom Questions and Workbooks.

Hamlet Scene by Scene Classroom Questions

Romeo and Juliet Scene by Scene Classroom Questions

King Lear Scene by Scene Classroom Questions

Macbeth Scene by Scene Classroom Questions

A Doll's House Classroom Questions

Animal Farm Classroom Questions

Foster Classroom Questions

Good Night, Mr. Tom Classroom Questions

Martyn Pig Classroom Questions

Of Mice and Men Classroom Questions

Pride and Prejudice Classroom Questions

Private Peaceful Classroom Questions

The Fault in Our Stars Classroom Questions

The Old Man and the Sea Classroom Questions

The Outsiders Classroom Questions

To Kill a Mockingbird Classroom Questions

The Spinning Heart Classroom Questions

Lightning Source UK Ltd.
Milton Keynes UK
UKHW021810130120
356877UK00007B/672/P